PHONICS CH

MT. VIEW ELEM.
Grade 2

Kids Care
about Sea
Animals

by Tim Johnson
Illustrations by Eileen Hine

Scholastic Inc.
New York   Toronto   London   Auckland   Sydney

Copyright © 1998 by Scholastic Inc.
Scholastic Phonics Chapter Books in design is a trademark of Scholastic Inc.
All rights reserved. Published by Scholastic Inc.
Printed in the U.S.A.
ISBN 0-590-03059-0

7 8 9 10   14   04 03 02 01 00

Dear Teacher/Family Member,

Scholastic Phonics Chapter Books provide early readers with interesting stories in easy-to-manage chapters. The books in this series are controlled for sounds and common sight words. Once sounds and sight words have been introduced, they are repeated frequently to give children lots of reading practice and to build children's confidence. When children experience success in reading, they want to read more, and when they read more, they become better readers.

Phonics instruction teaches children the way words work and gives them the strategies they need to become fluent, independent readers. However, phonics can only be effective when reading is meaningful and children have the opportunity to read many different kinds of books. Scholastic Phonics Chapter Books cover many curricular areas and genres. They are carefully designed to help build good readers, but more importantly, to inspire children to love reading.

Contents

Do you live near the sea? Have you ever visited a beach by the sea? Did you swim like a fish, or dive in the water like a sea bird?

Many animals live in or by the sea. Some are very small and some are very big. Some sea animals come onto the land near the water. Sea birds spend time on the beach, in the water, and fly in the sky over the sea.

In this book, you will find out how some sea animals get into trouble. You will find out why they sometimes need help from people. You will see what kids have done to try to help care for sea animals in trouble.

1 A Horseshoe Crab Came By

Can you tell what is crawling by, along this sandy beach? It looks like the hoof of a horse with a tail sticking out the back! But it is not a horse hoof!

This animal is called a horseshoe crab. It lives in the sea. It comes close to the beach to lay its eggs. It cannot stay on the beach for a long time. Soon it must go back to the sea.

A horseshoe crab has a thick shell. If you turned a horseshoe crab over, you would find tiny legs and claws. Sea birds like to eat those legs and claws.

A horseshoe crab must never flip over. Why? If it does, it cannot move and it is in trouble. A sea bird might fly down from the sky, try to grab it, and eat its legs and claws for lunch!

A wave has pushed this horseshoe crab onto the land. It needs to get back to the sea right away. It will try to quickly crawl back to the sea.

But then another strong wave comes along. Look what the wave has done! It has flipped the horseshoe crab over onto its back. The horseshoe crab is in trouble. If a sea bird comes by, it might try to eat the horseshoe crab. The sea bird might think, "That will be my lunch! What a picnic I will have!"

The crab will try and try to turn back over. But try as it might, it just will not flip. What will happen to it?

This horseshoe crab is in luck! A boy has come by and he sees the crab. The boy thinks the crab is in trouble.

The boy bends down and he sees the horseshoe crab's little legs and claws. The boy stops to help, but he wonders if the horseshoe crab will bite him. Then he remembers reading that horseshoe crabs do not bite! He will try to help.

The boy flips the horseshoe crab over with care. The horseshoe crab can now crawl back into the sea and be safe from the sea birds.

This boy helped the horseshoe crab. He didn't need money to help. He just needed to care, and he did.

What would you have done?

2 The Flight of the Puffins

Do you like birds? If so, you might like this one. It is called a puffin.

Puffins are sea birds. They spend most of their lives at sea. They eat fish and can dive deep into the water to catch them.

But puffins need to come on to land every spring to make nests and lay eggs. So when spring comes, puffins can be seen in high cliffs on the islands where they make their nests. It is quite a sight.

The puffins dig holes for their nests in the high cliffs. A puffin's bill is a good tool for digging. Each puffin will lay just one egg in its nest.

The puffins wait and wait on the island for the eggs to hatch. They wait in the daylight, and they wait at night.

Do you think they talk while they wait? They make sounds that might be like talking.

After six weeks go by, little puffin chicks hatch. They are called pufflings. Soon it is time for all the pufflings to fly from their cliff homes and go back to the sea.

Most pufflings fly from their nests in daylight, when they can see the water. Daytime is a good time to make the flight to the sea.

But pufflings that fly at night have a hard time. They can be fooled by the lights of a town and think that is where they need to go. No one can tell why pufflings are fooled, but sometimes they are.

A town is not a good place for sea birds that need water and fish. When pufflings fly to a town, it is quite a sight. Bright little pufflings can be seen everywhere. People who see them know they are in trouble. The pufflings are not in the right place and need help to get back to sea.

People who want to help them talk about what they might do. "Let's get some bags and boxes," says one boy. "We can use them to carry the pufflings when we take them back to sea."

Soon lots of people are there to help. Now, some of the pufflings are hiding. Kids, moms, and dads all help to find the pufflings.

Kids put the bright pufflings in bags and boxes and carry them with care. The little pufflings might not like this, but soon they will be just fine.

The children bring the bags and boxes to cars and trucks that will carry them to the beach.

When they come to the beach, the kids set the bags and boxes down. The pufflings fight to get out. The kids help set them free. Soon all the pufflings fly off. What a sight it is!

The kids talk about how they helped the pufflings. They know they did the right thing.

Do you think you might like to help care for pufflings someday?

⭐ 3 Every Child Can Help

Have you ever walked on a beautiful beach only to find trash in the sand? Trash on the sand is not a pretty sight. It is a danger to wild animals that live in and by the sea.

Many kinds of sea animals are harmed by trash. An animal may mistake the trash for food, eat it, and get sick. An animal may get trapped in the trash. Also, trash may bind an animal's neck. As the animal grows, the trash gets so tight that the animal cannot eat or breathe.

Even a child can help protect animals
from the danger of trash. Every year,
children work in teams to clean up beaches.
They put on gloves to protect their hands.
They find and pick up trash that may harm
sea animals.

Then one child fills out a card that says how much of each kind of trash they find. The teams save their cards from year to year. When they look at the cards, they can tell if there is more or less trash on the beach.

Each card says a lot about what kinds of trash the children find. Most of the trash is plastic, such as bags or the rings used to hold cans together. They find so much plastic because plastic lasts a long time. The plastic they find on beaches today may have been thrown away many years before.

Other kinds of trash that kids find are wood, paper, nets, and glass. Trash that winds up on the beach may come from far away.

Keep in mind, you do not have to be part of a team to show you care about animals in the wild. Here are some things you can do.

- Tell your friends how trash can harm sea animals. Talk about ways they can help keep wild sea animals safe.
- When you go to the beach, bring along a bag for trash. Don't leave trash behind.
- Ask a grown-up to help you clean up a beach. Put on your gloves and leave the beach more beautiful than you found it.

4 Whales at Low Tide

Do you know what the biggest animal in the sea might be? It is the whale.

Have you ever seen a whale? What do you know about whales?

Some people think a whale is a fish. But it is not. It is a mammal. A mother whale feeds her baby milk, just like cats, rabbits, and people do.

Whales eat lots and lots of food.
They find the food in deep water as they
swim about.

Did you know whales can sing
beautiful high-pitched songs and seem
to talk to other whales using the sounds
they make? To people, whale talk might
sound like someone is crying.

A whale's skin needs to stay wet at all times. That is why it swims in water. But every now and then a whale comes too close to the beach. If the tide is low, it can end up trapped on the dry sand.

What if you were taking a walk on the beach and saw a whale on the sand? How might you feel? A whale on the sand is a sad sight! Would you know what to do?

When a whale gets stuck on a beach at low tide, it is a time for kids, moms, and dads to pitch in and help protect it.

How can people help? At first, they might try to push the whale back into the water. But a whale is not light and it is much too big to push. So it is best to just let the whale stay right where it is until the tide comes in. When the tide is high, the whale can swim back out to sea.

How can a whale be kept safe until high tide?

To find out what to do, the people on the beach call someone for advice. She tells them to try to keep the whale's skin wet. The people use a hose to help keep the whale wet. Wet blankets can help too. The blankets keep the hot sun off the whale and help to keep its skin wet.

People watch as the whale lays there. They are very kind to the whale. They talk to it and rub its smooth skin. The kind people who are helping the whales are doing all they can to make the whale feel safe.

It must be very odd to be a beached whale. The whale must feel lost when out of the wild sea. It must wish so much to be back in the water, and wonder why it can't get there.

When the tide begins to roll in, the water gets deeper and deeper. The whale feels the cool sea water. It feels so good. The whale begins to move about, swishing its tail and fins.

The people help the whale turn the right way so it can swim. At long last, the water gets very deep and the whale can swim off.

"How beautiful the whale is," says one child. "I'm glad we were here when the tide came in. I'm glad the whale is free."

"I know," says another child. "It makes me feel good to know that I helped the whale. I hope it will have a long life in the wild."

"How kind you kids are for the care you gave the whale when it needed help," says a dad.

"When you walk on this beautiful beach
in the days to come, you will always
remember how kind you were. You will
know that you did the right thing at the right
time," a mom adds.

In this book, you are reading about
the animals you see on this map.
Look for each of the animals.

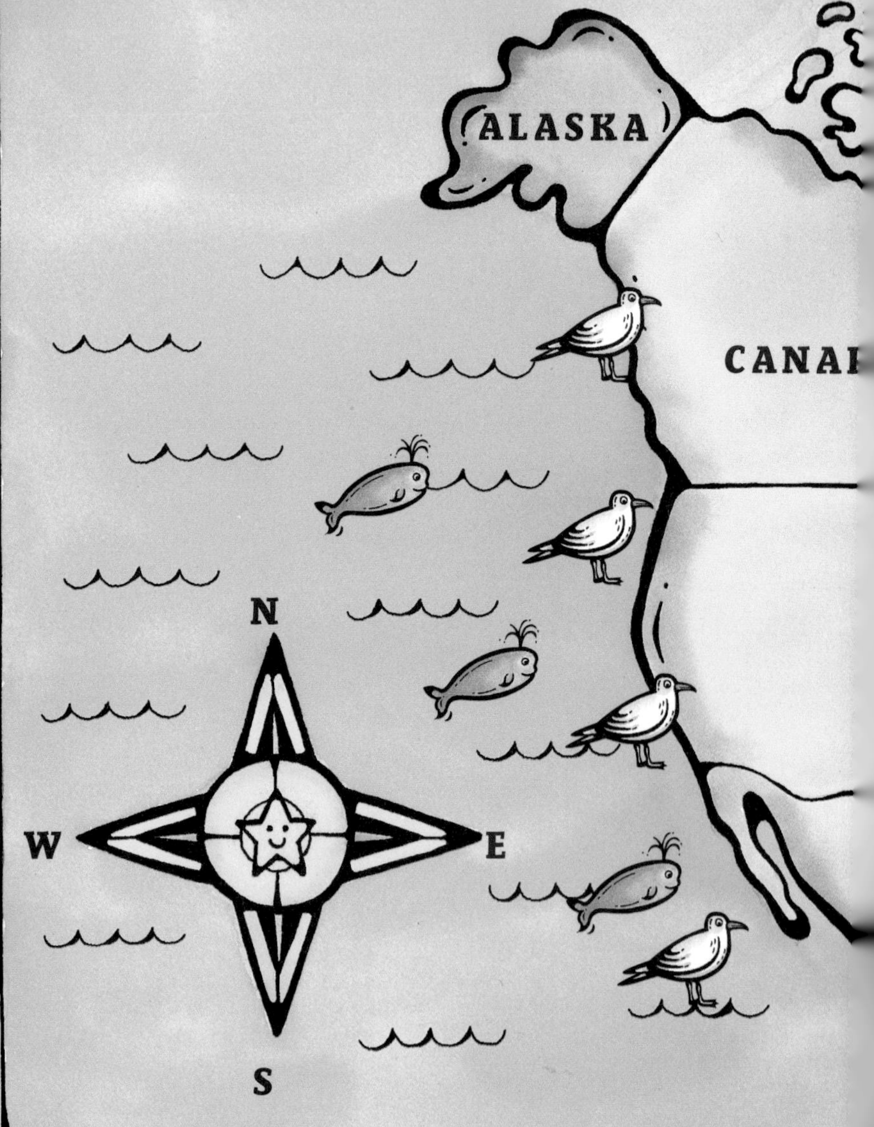

ALASKA

CANA[...]

N

W   E

S

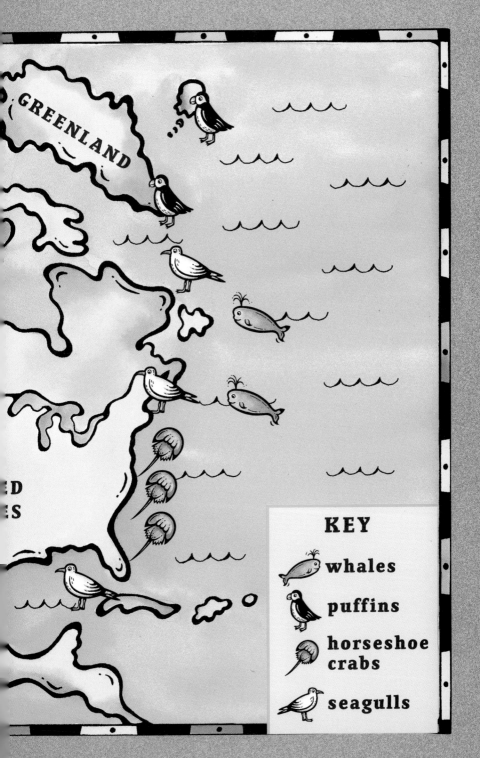

GREENLAND

KEY

whales

puffins

horseshoe crabs

seagulls

29

There are animals all over the world that might need your care.

Why do animals sometimes need help? They need us to protect the places where they live. They need us to make sure they have the food they need to live.

You might read about what you can do to help care for sea animals near where you live. You might someday show that you are a kid who cares.

Find out about some of these animals:

dolphins

otters

manatees

Decodable Words With the Phonic Elements

1 y

by	sky
fly	try
my	why

2 igh

bright	lights
daylight	might
fight	night
flight	right
high	sight

3

-ind	-ild
behind	child
bind	wild
find	
kind	
mind	
winds	

4 review

y	-ind
crying	find
dry	kind
try	
why	-ild
	child
igh	wild
high	
light	
might	
right	
sight	